ONE OF THE LOST SOULS

Order this book online at www.trafford.com
or email orders@trafford.com

Most Trafford titles are also available at major online book retailers.

Printed in the United States of America.

ISBN: 978-1-5539-5044-8 (sc)

Trafford rev. 02/13/2012

 www.trafford.com

North America & international
toll-free: 1 888 232 4444 (USA & Canada)
phone: 250 383 6864 ♦ fax: 812 355 4082

ONE OF THE LOST SOULS,
THE JOURNAL OF AN ABUSED CHILD
BY
DANIELLE X

DEDICATIONS

TO 'BLACK JACK': REST IN PEACE

TO MOOKIE: MY WORLD, MY LIFE, MY REASON FOR LIVING.

TO IDA MAE: THE ONLY PERSON WHO REALLY CARED.

TO ANITRA: CAUSE YOU SCRATCHED MY HEAD WHEN I WAS AILING.

INTRODUCTION

Some one once asked me... Who am I?...Who am I, you ask? And what will they say about me when I'm gone? Who gives a care? My miserable little life? I'm nobody. I'm at a crossroads in my life, I can't tell my face from my backside. Everything I do falls on one side. I'm sick of my dead end life, with a dead end job. I was led to believe, by my grandmother that I was a born loser. I'm lost, I don't know where I'm supposed to be. I didn't choose this life or this world, I guess this is just the way things are supposed to be.

I'm thirty-one year's old, I have a ten year old son. I'm a black single mother with homosexual tendencies, I've always been afraid to say I was gay. I don't feel gay, to admit that sounds so final. What I can say is that, I prefer the companionship of a woman. Not that I can compare that to a man, I've never been in a relationship with a man. How can I have a child without having had a relationship with a man? Sex does not necessarily mean an emotional commitment. It's not the dick that I don't want, it's what's attached to the dick that I can't deal with.

I believe my attraction for women started as a child when I longed for my mother's presence. As a child I didn't know the difference between my need for a nurturing female figure and sexual desires. The more the men in my life mistreated me, the more I wanted a woman's love. I've never filled the void that my mother left.

I've spent the last eleven year's of my life high. Yes, I'm a drug user. No, I don't rob or steal for my high. I don't degrade myself for my high. I am not a traditional junkie. Some wouldn't even consider weed a serious drug. But I believe anything you have to have on a daily basis, is a habit. I really didn't think it was a problem until I took a long look at my life.

My drug of choice is marijuana. I have tried cocaine, acid, wet and "x". I've never touched crack, heroine or meth. It doesn't make me feel any better. I don't 'lose' my life when I'm high. I smoke weed like other people smoke cigarettes.

I'm not a perfect person, but I do have a good heart. I'm at a point in my life where sometimes, I feel like I can't go on. But then I think about my son. What would he do without me? I often feel like he would be better off without me. But, the reality of it is, he does need me, so I can't give up.

My life hasn't been all peaches and cream. But it could be worse. I watch the news everyday and it troubles me. It's so much going on today...murder, violence, drugs and child molestation. When does it end? The world has become a very sick place and if we don't change the cycle, we will eventually self-destruct.

I grew up in the church and the things they were teaching and preaching about, they were not living about. Religion has become very confusing to me. Who's right? Who's going to heaven?...Who gives a shit? With everything that is going on around us, who can worry about the hereafter? I gave up on religion along time ago. I believe in God, don't get me wrong, I just think God doesn't like to get his hands dirty. I feel he gives us the basics and we have to learn on our own. I thank god for my life, however miserable it is. I can hear, I can see, I can walk and I'm breathing. And for that, I am thankful. Life is like a card game, you can't help the cards you're dealt, and you just have to play your hand. And a miserable hand I've been dealt. From a child up until now. I look back at my life and wonder why. I wonder will my life ever be on a positive track.

My Aunt Ida says that everything happens for a reason. That everything is predestined. Then that allows me to believe, as my grandmother told me year's ago, my family was cursed. She didn't say my family on my father's side, because that is the side

4

that she commanded. But my mother's side, which was, in her eyes, filled with bad spirits and curses. A life of booze, drugs and good times. It may not be the best life, but by what authority could she judge my family? Because my father's side went to church regularly? Nobodies perfect. Religion doesn't make you higher or mightier than the next person. I believe a Christian should be a loving and caring person, and shouldn't have hate in his heart. My 'save' family watched for years, as I was beat and neglected. Not once coming to my aid. Where's the love? But as I got older and begin going in the wrong direction, they took it upon themselves to judge me.

I am the oldest of approx. fifteen children. I have a relationship of some sort with three or four of them. I am close to just one, because we suffered together. I was stripped of my right to a relationship with my siblings, by my neglectful, immature parents. My mother, God rest her soul, had too many children by too many different men. As if that wasn't enough, she gave us all away to different people. We were all involved in various situations that had a negative impact of some sort on our life. Not to say we aren't fine now, but life wasn't easy for us. My youngest brother, for instance, doesn't know his father. I hear people say all the time, a lot of us don't know our father. I'm not using that as an excuse. But we need to stop acting like that is normal. Not knowing your father is not normal. We should stop accepting that way of life.

My brother was giving away to a couple of that had drinking problems, God rest their souls, I'm just keeping it real. They loved him dearly, but an everyday drunk isn't capable of taking care of himself, let alone a small child. My mother was a heavy alcohol abuser while carrying him, thus his medical and developmental problems. His adoptive parents died when he was thirteen.

Some people were interested in keeping him until they found out that his adoptive mom didn't have a hefty insurance policy. But I felt obligated to take care of him with or without a life insurance policy. I didn't know what the hell I was doing. I was only twenty-four myself. I didn't understand how he felt, being snatched from the only home he knew and placed in a home with his older sister, who he thought was his cousin, for years. He actually found out that my mother was his mother, by a stranger on the city bus. He's been selling crack and smoking weed since the age of ten. He wouldn't behave in school at all. He was kicked out of every school in the district. I gave him an ultimatum, school or work!

My workday was interrupted every week, I was tired. Tired of the meetings with his principal. Tired of having to take time off work to discuss his nonsense behavior. Of course he blames me for his being a fuck up! He says it's my fault he didn't graduate and doesn't have a job. It wasn't my fault, where was his mother? His father? Brought into this world with no regard to his survival, just another lost soul.

The third youngest child, a survivor, taught at a very young age, that no one was going to take care of her, but her. A born hustler, struggling to stay alive. She would steal the ring from around your collar, it was the only way she knew. No one was giving her anything she wanted or anything she needed. She had to steal to survive. Because I never bonded with my sisters, I felt no loyalty towards them. This caused me to betray this sister, when we were younger. I was so wrapped up in the life, I didn't regard my sister's feelings. I don't blame anyone but myself. I do believe if we would have had opportunities to bond like real sisters, things would have turned out differently. We have since put the past behind us. I trust she knows that I love her very much, and would never do anything to hurt her ever again. I am most proud of this sibling, she took nothing and turned it into something.

The sister I'm close with was conceived in love, but punished by hatred. This sister and I are the only ones with the same father. I will from now on refer to her as my full sister. We were both mistreated and abused. She reminds me of my mother. My sister thought what she was looking for, she'd find with no good men. That behavior left her with different children by different men. I don't blame her for that. I love my nieces and my nephews, very deeply. What makes me respect her is that she knows her children and they know her. I'm happy she didn't give them all away. I can honestly say this sibling and I were punished for our mother's sins.

My second half-sister, in my eyes, was conceived in a sickening manner. All those year's, all those lies. We were brought up as cousins. I knew she was my sister. We were jealous of her, we thought she thought she was better then us. We had no clue.

And then there's me, the first born. We were all denied our family, denied the chance to bond, denied our mother's love.

I stayed mostly with my father and grandmother, I believe they thought they were doing the right thing. As a child I thought they were keeping me from my mother. I don't know much about my mother, mostly rumors and speculations. After she left me and went to Smithville, all I knew is what other people told me.

We act as if children don't matter. Everything you do or expose a child to affects that child in some way or another. The problems around today are some of the same problems we had yesterday. Children are being ignored, like they don't have feelings. Children are being abused and mistreated. We're going in circles. We must somehow break the chain and change our future. Because our children, are our future.

I've tried to take a long look at my life and figure out where it went wrong. I don't want people to misunderstand me or to judge me without knowing, what I've been through, where I've come from, how I got here. I wish I could go back and figure out when and where I lost my soul, and what I need to do to find it. Could it have been when my mother left me or the day I was born.

THE BEGINNING

I often wonder when my mother left me. It seems like forever, because I never remember her being there. All those lonely years without someone to comfort me, protect me, love me. I was the very first born. I was told I was a pretty baby with no hair. Innocent and unwanted. Unwanted by my father, he was in no way ready to have a child. He was young and wild. There were so many things he hadn't seen yet. Unwanted by my mother, who could barely take care of herself.

Coming from a broken home and not having a family bond, I felt alone all my life. I felt as if no one wanted me or loved me. I was born in a very small town by the beach. I was told my mother had come from a broken home too, which made me feel as if I was destined for the same way of life. My mother was very familiar with the 'street' side of life. Drugs, alcohol and good times. My father was from a whole entirely different side of life. Choir rehearsal and 'ypww' meetings. That's not saying he wasn't in the streets, because he had seen the streets and he knew what they looked like. He had a religious background and a supposedly 'structured' life. His 'sanctified' mother would never allow him to be with the likes of my mother. My paternal grandmother felt like my mother was a whore, and that my mother's mother was a whore. That may or may not have been true. She said my maternal grandmother's babies were cursed. She didn't mind telling me that from time to time, when I was a child. She kept reminding me, like I had forgotten since the last time she had told me.

The pressures of her life were too much on my mother. Because she couldn't take care of a child by herself, she married my father. She had no choice. She thought he would take care of her. He promised.

My father, who I've heard, was forced to marry my mother by his father and grandfather. How honorable. I don't believe my father was ready for marriage either. They started the whole marriage thing off wrong. Three weeks after having me, my mother went back to work.

I heard she tried to be a good wife and mother. But the weight of life, and being married to an asshole with a gorilla/beast mentality, made it quite difficult. I don't know when the ass whippings started, I just remember them happening. My mother's life was horrible and getting worse. She probably wanted to die. Her mean husband had caveman potential. Her mother-in-law, God rest her soul, hated her. My grandmother was a very scary woman. If you didn't know any better you'd think she practiced voodoo secretly. The spirits were always talking to her. I don't remember much of the life I had with my mother and father together. Just faint memories. I remember one time they were in the room with the door closed. My mother was making moaning noises. I knew what they were doing. I also remember my father beating my mother. I can remember beating the broom on the living room wall. Beckoning my great-grandmother, to the aid of my mother. I felt like I was rescuing my mother.

"Baby.." My great-grandmother
said. She always smelt like asthma
medicine. She had asthma really
bad.
"Yes grandmother?" I said.
"Next time your daddy's beating
your mama, you beat that broom
and grandmother will come, okay?"
"Okay grandmother."

My great-grandmother would come every time. She was a very loving and caring woman, but her age and chronic asthma, would limit what she could do. I cared for her deeply. She was one of the few people that showed me any love. I can remember going to her mailbox on Saturday mornings and finding a shiny quarter just for me. She walked with a strut and her skirt tail popped every time she took a step. My great-grandmother was always humming something.

I can't imagine walking in my mother's shoes, her life was so unbearable. She was a baby taking care of a baby. She was only seventeen. My grandmother was a mess. She put my mother and I out, we had no where to stay. My mother ended up moving in with a friend in her trailer. The trailer was already full with this ladies children. She was kind enough to let us stay. This ladies children were among the first to molest me. Right under my mother's nose. Sometimes I wonder why no one saw what was going on.

My mother had no food and no money. She had to do something so we could eat. This friend, and I use friend lightly, suggested my mother do the unspeakable. So in her most desperate time of need, she demonstrated the highest example of a mother's love for her child. She did this so she could feed me. My mother was in over her head. What was she thinking? Someone told my father. He beat her like never before. Off to Chicago she went.

Although my mother and father were too young to be married and not ready for commitment. It was believed that they had a true love for one another.

They decided, despite the problems seen and unseen, to give it another go. They tried but they failed. My mother ended up with more bruises and another baby. I once witnessed my father kicking my mother in the stomach when she was pregnant with my full sister. He had on some brown zip up boots with the stack heels. Every time I hear Sly Stone's 'babies making babies', it reminds me of that moment. I was young, very young, but I remember that clearly.

His meanness and physical abuse were worse than ever and the hate my grandmother had for my mother was stronger and harder than ever. I really can't blame my grandmother because she loved her son and she had heard rumors of a half-white baby. I guess my grandmother didn't think about the position she put my mother in, in the first place. My mother had no self-esteem and no self-love. When they realized that they were not going to make this work, they split up...forever. I had no where to go. My mother took my younger sister with her. She left me. My mother didn't want me, my father didn't either. No rejection feels worse, than that from your mother. It wasn't my fault that my mother left me. I felt like my grandmother held me responsible for my mother's shortcomings. She told me every chance she could that my family was no good and that I wasn't going to be any good either.

"Them Jackson women is cursed!" She said. "You ain't go be nothing!" She said, with her nose turned up like she was better than everybody.

My mother's life was out of control. She had three kids and no one to help her. It's difficult for me and I have only one child and no help, I can only imagine what it's like with three. The life of drugs, alcohol and good times, gave her temporary relief from her troubled soul. I was told that the city lights had her mesmerized.

My father was in a destructive rut of his own. He wasn't at peace with himself. He too had seeds scattered abroad. Four children by three different women. He ran right into the marines. He came back even meaner then he was when he left.

A GIFT FROM GOD

I spent the next couple of years of my life with a lady that was first introduced to me, at the very, very young age of three weeks. She babysat me when my mother had to go back to work so soon after my birth. She had only been in town six months prior to my being born. She's my unbreakable spirit. She was running from an abusive husband. She had been mistreated and violently beaten. She had to run for her life, she was scared he would kill her.

My Aunt Ida was a kind but stern lady. I say 'was' because her grandchildren have made her soft. She wasn't affectionate when I was little, but she was a good provider and a great cook. She was exactly what I needed, stability. I grew up believing my Aunt Ida was the only one that loved me. There were always hot meals and clean clothes. When other people wanted to throw me away, Aunt Ida stood fast.

"She's just an innocent child!" My Aunt Ida said, "she needs love too!"
"I wouldn't keep her, Sista Ida!" Her sister said, "It ain't worth the trouble!"

Aunt Ida's sister was initially supposed to be my godmother. I don't know what happened I just bonded better with Aunt Ida, I guess. Her sister wasn't lying, because it was nothing but trouble. To have someone playing in my panties, or sticking their privates in my mouth occurred often. It happened at Aunt Ida's sisters' house. When her son's babysat me. I was only fondled by the eldest son. He was young too, maybe eight-year's older than I. He didn't know he was messing my head up. He never penetrated me, but he fingered me on many occasions. I was six or seven. That was as violating as if he would have gone all the way.

Even when I visited my mother and sister in Smithville. That's where a good bit of the sexual abuse took place. My mother didn't even see it. My mother had become a heavy drinker. My full sister and I were under the impression that being violated was a normal thing. Once, even fighting over whom was the girlfriend of our mother's male friend. He was babysitting us. We also were fighting over who was going to perform oral sex on him first. I was seven and my sister was four. Fighting over a grown man in his boxers with an erect penis, in the dark bedroom. We should have been in the living room, with the lights on! That nigga should have had on some cat-pickin' pants!

There was another time when my sister and I were home, this man, I don't remember who he was o where he came from. I guess the man came over to see my mother, but was distracted by the smell of fresh young girl.

I was walking down the cold hallway. I had to be bare footed cause I can remember the floor being cold. I heard some noises coming from the bathroom, the light was on and the door was cracked. I peeped in the door, I seen this fat man. I thought he was using the bathroom. He was standing in front of the toilet. I pushed the door open slowly, so he wouldn't hear me. Something wasn't right, I could just feel it. As I pushed the door open more, I could see the man wasn't alone. My little sister was straddling the toilet, the fat man in front of her. My sister was young and not knowing any better tried to scoot down and assist this old pervert with penetrating her. She was four or five year's old.

"Oh my God!" I couldn't believe my
eyes!! Although this wasn't my
first sexual encounter, I had never

seen that before.
"Get your little ass out of here!" He
told me.
"I'm telling mama!" I was so scared,
I could hardly move, I had a
rock in my gut that made my
feet heavy.

The terror in my sisters big, brown eyes gave me
enough strength to close the door and go get my
mother. I shook my mother real hard. She didn't know
if it was a dream or reality. I shook my mother again,
real hard this time.

"Mama, Mama?.." I yelled.
"What?" My mother yelled back,
I think she was pissed because
I was waking her up.
"Mama!" I yelled again
"What?..." my mother said, "...what
the fuck do you want?"
"That man's in there doing it to my
sister!" I told her
"What?.." My mother said, "..oh,
my God!"

My mother was now fully awake, and had that
same rock in her gut that I had in mine. My mother
had been drinking and didn't know if she was coming
or going. She didn't know what to do. She scrambled

around in the dark room until she came to a Kentucky fried chicken box. It had some salt, hot sauce, napkins and a plastic fork. My mother grabbed the plastic fork, into the hallway she went. I stayed behind in the bedroom and only stuck my head out to see.

"Nigga, what the fuck you doing?" My mother asked him. She was staggering around the hall. She had that plastic fork cocked like it was an eight-inch blade. I was so nervous, I had to shit. "Fuck you, bitch!" the pervert said. Him and my mother scuffled. After throwing my mother around a little bit the molester left.

My mother slammed the door behind him. The nerve of him he was pissed at my mother and he was in the wrong. For the moment we felt safe. We didn't talk much about the incident. To this day my sister is embarrassed by it, I still feel the same way I did when I walked in on it. We must have had 'public sex toys' stamped on our forehead. It was like a molester's union. Someone must have passed our name out, every molester knew he or she could do it to us.

Molester's come in both sexes. No matter how protective my Aunt Ida was, even she couldn't be there to protect me all the time. Aunt Ida took me to Smithville for my Aunt's funeral. We stayed with Aunt

Ida's cousins. Her cousin had two children, a son and a daughter; Adam and Eve. We arrived for the funeral a day early. I was very sad because I really loved my Aunt. I can remember helping her clean her arm up to take her insulin shots. I knew I would miss her. That night after the funeral Aunt Ida, Aunt Ida's sister and me went back to the house. We were going to leave the next morning. It was only an hour and a half drive. In the bedroom where I was to sleep, there were two twin beds. One by the window and one by the door. Aunt Ida's other cousin, Sylvia slept by the window. Sylvia didn't attend the funeral, although she traveled to Smithville with us. Eve shared a bed with me. We slept by the door. I can remember feeling accepted because she wanted me to sleep with her. As I felt special by the attention, I had no idea what she had in store for me.

We started the night off with me at the foot. Eve was at the head of the bed. I was lying in the bed, sadden by the fact that my mother didn't want me. How did I know that at such a young age? I was too young to understand, but I knew. I knew because my grandmother had told me. She had also taken it upon herself to tell me about my mother's half-white baby. That devastated me. I cried myself to sleep.

Eve woke up in the wee hour of the morning. She begin to fondle me, and made me fondle her. When I had completely woke up, Eve had her fingers in my vagina. I can remember how uncomfortable I was. It hurt me, I squeezed my eyes tight, thinking she would stop soon. She didn't. I told her she was hurting me and I was going to get into the bed with Sylvia. She told me that Sylvia would whip me if I woke her up. I was too young too see the manipulation. She began to put me between her legs, pulling my body up against her vagina. She wasn't fresh, she smelled of old fish. I find it odd that I can remember such details. Aunt Ida tells me, my behavior was not quite right the next morning. She had noticed the stains from Eve's body fluids on my t-shirt. Aunt Ida says they didn't know what was wrong with me. Eve knew. And her brother Adam knew. Adam had just violated me a few months earlier. He had made me perform oral sex on him. He had taken it upon himself to misuse my innocence. I can remember the stale, salty taste his thing left in my mouth. I could prove I had seen his thing, I knew he had a mole on the side of it. How could I have known that, unless I had seen it? I could have told someone. Tell whom? No one would believe me. People said my mother and I were whores. I believed I was a whore. I was scared, and then I began to get angry. I can remember Adam looking at me, as if, he knew what I was thinking. He dropped his head. We finished breakfast and returned to New Port. I was seven and a half-year's old.

FAMILY REUNION

It was summer 1978, my father was out of the marines. With an empty promise of a birthday party, he lured my sister from my mother. To be honest, she was actually better off with my father then she would have been with my mother. My father and grandmother weren't as hard on my sister as they were on me. But my sister had endured enough by the age of five that would have a negative impact on her for the rest of her life.

My full sister was glad to be back with our father. The fast life my mother was living, was no way for a child to live.

My father had also gotten me from my Aunt Ida. We lived with my father's mother. Things weren't terrible with my grandmother, she just had a hateful way of talking to you. Besides the verbal abuse, not having clean clothes, listening to them constantly bad mouth my mother and not having much to eat, it wasn't that bad at all...right! She never laid a finger on me. She did whip my sister when she shit in the tub. No sexual abuse ever took place in my grandmother's home. Our daily meals were either grits or peanut butter & jelly sandwiches. My uncle that lived in the house with us once made up a song.

"Grits in the morning, grits in the
evening, grits at suppertime!" He
would sing, he would sing it like
a country and western song.

But, I guess you could say; we could have been hungry. We were thankful for that.

I was glad to be with my sister, but with her return came issues. All the sexual abuse and neglect shined through, coming out in her behavior. I kept an eye on her all the time, I felt like I had to protect her. I would come in the room where my sister was alone, and find my younger sister fondling herself. Grinding on furniture, clothes, her fists, cabinet doors and crayons. I chastised her whenever I caught her.

"Where your hands at?" I would
ask her.
"Right here." She would say and
hold her hands up, so her big

do that to my little sister?
them? For God's sake she
as I tried I couldn't fix what
r. The damage had already
been done to the both of us
behavior was altered, our
ual abuse. If my father and
e paid attention to the signs, if
centrating on all the mistakes
e, they could have made a
They just made things worse.
I us sometimes. It started out
Mama would ride down with her
d four children in a small town
ew Port. We had a good time
visit us. We got a chance to play
ey smoked a lot of weed, drunk a
would play and dance. I was
ive then my sister. Always crying
it never failed, I would cry every
er.

e stay with you?" I asked.
I was better off without

ster's   ght now.." she said,
ould   nfort me.
was   s crying!" My sister said,

she was dancing like a go-go dancer on soul train.

"I don't wanna stay with grandma and daddy!" I said. The small trailer was in an uproar, music blasting, weed smoke everywhere.

"Stop crying!" My sister said, trying to cheer me up. "Let's dance!" By now my sister is standing on the coffee table.

"Get down, Sissie, get down.." My mother was cheering my sister on, my full sister thought she was grooving.

"Okay mama.." My sister said, my sister thought my mother meant get down, as in 'get yo ass off the furniture' down.

"No, no, Sissie." Mama said, she put my sister back on the table.

"I mean, get doowwnn!" Mama started doing something like the funky chicken. My sister was dancing so hard and so fast, she look like she was going to shake herself right off the table.

I was so wrapped up and overjoyed by my si dancing, I was dancing too. Hell, I figured if she dance on the table and not get in trouble, that I going to dance too.

"Get down, get down with yo' bad
self!" We all said, "get down with
yo' bad self!" I can't remember
us ever having that much fun before.
That was the last time.

My mother's visits didn't come as often. We wanted to go with our aunt anyway. Our father and grandmother wouldn't let us. Soon after that, she would say she was coming but never did. We would sit up all night, with our garbage bags packed. Yes...garbage bags. 11pm, 12am, 1am and no mama. We would run to the window every time the car lights from passing cars would shine in the house. It was like my father and grandmother got a kick out of that. Anything to make my mother look bad. They had no idea how that affected us. They had no idea what was going on with our mother. They didn't care how that hurt us either. The last time I remember my mother trying to visit us my father wouldn't let her. I remember my mother riding up with her man friend. My father had promised me that if my mother wanted us, we could leave with her that day. My father went out to the car and wouldn't let me follow him out. He wouldn't allow me to see my own mother. I stood in the window as my parents talked. They talked, it turned into an argument and my father pushed her back into the car. My father came back into the house.

"She don't want you!" He said, "she rather drink!"

"That's not true..." I said, "..Mama loves us!"

"No she don't, shut up!" He said.

I would not dare say another word. I was terrified of my father. He probably was right by not letting us go with her. I wouldn't let my son go with his father, if he was sloppy drunk. We were children, we didn't understand. I just felt like my mean daddy wouldn't let us go with our mother. He left the house and slammed the door. I went and stood in the back room of the house...and started crying. My sister has always tried to be tough, and act like she didn't care. She cared, that may have just been her way of dealing with it.

When we were children, my sister and I, we were not allowed to take up for our mother. Any time we expressed our feelings about missing our mother or disagreeing with what they were saying, we got beat. We stopped expressing ourselves for fear of getting beat. From experience I'm saying; this is devastating to a child. Which part? All of it.

BETRAYAL

My sister had learned a little survival tip 'if you can't beat em', join em'". If she spent her time talking about our mother, she could get on their good side. My sister began blaming me for everything. Joining in with the negative comments about our mother and her life style. Anything to keep the bad attention away from her. I really don't blame her, who would want those ass whippings? And get talked about like a dirty dog. I felt like everybody was against me. Including an uncle, who was only a few years older than me. I believe he talked my father into giving me at least 50% of the beatings I got. My uncle was always saying 'man you need to beat her!' He thought that was funny. It was not funny. Between my grandmother's verbal assaults, my sister's disloyalty to our mother, my uncle's taunts and my father's physical abuse, I was miserable! All of this was too much for me. I was only eight and carried the burdens of an adult.

My uncle had a strange ability to manipulate his older brother. Not manipulating him into doing undesired things, nor did he use this ability to obtain material things. My father had low self-esteem and was slightly paranoid. My uncle knew this, he knew exactly how to push my father's buttons.

My sister and I were sleeping in the bedroom across from the kitchen. My father and uncle sat at the dining room table. What once was a playful brotherly discussion had turned into a heated argument. My uncle had gotten my father upset. He was always talking shit. He got a kick out of pissing other people off. My father, in a wild violent rage grabbed an extension cord and began to beat me in my sleep. Yelling and sounding like a wild cave man.

"You been talking about me?" My
father asked, "huh?" Swinging hard
as he could. My uncle was cracking
up. I wanted to scream 'it ain't
funny!'. My little sister was so
scared. She was terrified, she later
told me she that felt sorry for me, but
was glad it wasn't her.
"That's enough Nat!" my grandmother told him. I think that was
the only time she took up for me.

"Man, Nat..." my uncle said, shaking his head, "..You crazy!" He just laughed, I still didn't know what was so funny. "That's for what you go do!" My daddy said, smirking.

I hated him, I hated that house, I hated my mother and I hated myself. My legs and back were whelped and bleeding and nobody cared. My uncle told my father that I had been talking about him to Aunt Ida. Aunt Ida would never allow that type of disrespect. She may have said something; she didn't allow me to. She always taught me to love my mother and father anyway. I hadn't even seen Aunt Ida. I hated my existence, I was almost nine year's old and wished I were dead.

My father and grandmother were so wrapped up in casting out the bad spirits in me, that they didn't even see what was going on with my sister. Were they blind? Her behavior...you could tell someone had been molesting her. I caught her one time trying to do it to a boy in a wheel chair. I wanted to tell on her, but I didn't. I didn't wish those beatings on anybody. Not even my little sister, who helped in my mistreatment.

Sometimes they allowed my Aunt Ida to keep me. When it was convenient and benefited them. I found refuge with Aunt Ida. When they sent me with no shoes or too little shoes, she would always send me back with new ones. Aunt Ida loved me like I was her own. But, she couldn't protect me from the cruelty of the children who knew I was unwanted and a throwaway. The kids use to beat me up, chase me home, take my lunch money and one child pushed me, face first, into a glass storm door. I still have the scar on my nose. The grown-ups treated me like an outcast, like a liar and a thief. I was only a child, God knows that I didn't deserve that. I know I did things that I am ashamed of, as I got older. But when I was that age, I wasn't doing all the things I was accused of. I was a child that needed to be loved and have someone stand up for me.

NEW FAMILY

My father finally found a woman crazy enough to marry him. My 1st stepmother...sounds funny? I had about five or six of them. Anyway, my 1st stepmother was a pretty woman, bright yellow skin, pretty brown eyes. When I first met her I liked her. I had begun to have these strange feelings. As a child I yearned for my mother's nurturing. I was too young to know the difference between love and sex. Introduced to sex way too early, I thought I was having a sexual desire for a woman. My misunderstanding of the desires for a woman's touch turned into lesbian desire. I never acted on it, I didn't even know what it was. I just knew that was the way I was feeling, I thought about it all the time. It turned into my fantasy and I used my fantasies as an escape from what was going on around me. I thought I had a secret crush on her, but I just wanted her to love me. Everything else in my life was black and ugly, but not my stepmother. She was hot, in a Claire Huxtable kind of way. My sister hated her. We both found it difficult to call her mama. So we settled on ma'.

I would soon grow to dislike her too. My father's mistreatment of her aided in my dislike. My stepmother, who was being beat and mistreated, took her anger for her husband out on us.

My 1st stepmother had a daughter from a previous relationship. She and my full sister were close in age. We all got along pretty well. There were an endless number of nights when we were awakened by violent screams.

"Help, help!". She would scream, "he's
choking me!", she was always
screaming that. "Help!", at our cousins
house, "help!", at my grandmother's
house. She even screamed at her own
house. "Break a window, he's trying to
kill me!"
"Ya'll better not say shit!" he would say.

We were scared, we wouldn't have helped her even if we knew how. Even her own daughter was too scared to help.

My stepmother had a little boy soon after that. It was my father's fifth or sixth child. That didn't change anything, he was still mean as a rattlesnake. The things he would do to my little brother. He once locked him in the bedroom naked, with his dog, Scooby. Scooby was a Great Dane, big scary ass dog. As the dog barked, my little brother screamed and my father laughed. My father got a sick kick out of terrorizing his children.

My stepmother did her best, she tried to be a good wife. She was taking care of two children that weren't any of hers. I remember her cooking and cleaning. But with my father's cheating and physical abuse, she couldn't take too much more. In her absence, he would throw parties and had women sitting on her couch, drinking from her glasses. By the way, her absence was due to her giving birth to a second child, a girl. No matter how he treated her, he demanded his respect, and she dare defy him. As his treatment of her worsened, so did her treatment of his children. I didn't understand then, but I still had pity for her. Because I too had been an object of his brutality. I also forgave her for being mean to us, cause when my father was beating her, he wasn't beating me. I felt like she was taking the beatings that were meant for me.

He treated the new baby girl really nice. I think he liked her most of all. I use to watch as he held her in the palm of his hands, her little feet and legs dangling down his wrist. But having affection for a baby doesn't make up for the mistreatment of its mother. My stepmother grew tired and maybe a little afraid for her life, the same way my mother did. She even went as far as, cooking up a little remedy that would take care of my father once and for all.

"Ma?..." I said, "...can I have some grits?"
"Naaww.." she said, "...you don't want none of them grits!" she smirked.

My stepmother had made breakfast with a secret ingredient. Pine-sol, my bad, Lysol. That may not have killed him, but it sure as hell would have given him the shits. My grandmother came over and tried to pray with them, make things better. That nigga needed some medicine not prayer! He was crazy. Maybe a little prayer wouldn't have hurt. Things didn't get any better, things got worse.

During the time my dad was with his second-wife, was the closest we ever came to a normal family. We were always in competition with our stepsister, at least trying to be. We were young and just being children. I hated the way she would stick her fingers in all of the oatmeal. We always got a whipping when she got in trouble, but not the other way around.

I can remember being kind of mean to her though. We did cruel things, like we gave her some chocolate x-lax before. It was hilarious.

We went to visit my mother's godmother, which was something we wanted for ourselves only. She wasn't our real sister. But we were kids, we did what we were told. So, my stepsister had to come. Anyway, we gave her this x-lax, my stepsister's stomach began to hurt. We got tickled, we knew what we had done. She went into the bathroom and boy, it was do-do everywhere. My mother's godmother was a Christian lady, didn't curse much...unless you pissed her off. My sister and I knew exactly how to do that. To see her upset and nervous was entertaining for the two of us. My stepsister's bowels were tore-up, she made a mess of the bathroom.

"Oh my god, child!" The old lady
said, "what's wrong with you?"
My sister and I were laughing so
loud. "You gonna help me clean
this toilet!" she yelped. She gave
her the toilet brush, my stepsister knew nothing about cleaning, but tried anyway. "What's
wrong with you?", we were laughing so hard, we were crying.
"Girl, don't you see that shit all over?"
My god-grandmother was
getting frustrated now, we
couldn't stop laughing. "Get
that shit! Look at all that shit in
that bowl!" She grabbed the toilet
brush, "What the hell is so funny?"
she yelled, "Get outta here, I'm
taking ya'll home!!"

My sister and I managed to run her blood pressure up...again. It didn't matter though, she loved our mother so she put up with us. No matter how many times we pissed her off, she still came to visit and did things for us. She used to oversee some blueberry fields. We used to go pick berries with her a lot. We'd run her crazy every time.

Every since I was a child I could always tell when something bad was going to happen. This one time we went to the blueberry fields, something wasn't right, I could feel it. We always stayed for hours and it was always too hot. I was picking slow, when I think about it, I was always picking slow. Then I had something like a vision, I seen my little brother's potty-chair being thrown across the living room.

"Danielle!" my sister yelled, breaking my dream. "What's wrong with you?" she said. I didn't say a word. "Fool!", she said and started picking again.

"I've got a feeling, some bodies gonna get into a fight!" I said. My sister joined in, she had this uncanning ability to turn everything she sang, into a church song.

"I've got a feeling, some bodies going to get into a fight!!" My sister was now summoning me to harmonize. I had completely forgotten what I had seen and started in with my crazy sister. My sister was so animated. She always tried to cheer me up. "Oh my lord, oh my lord, some bodies going to get into a fight!"

My god-grandmother was so glad it was time to take us home, she was always glad to see us coming and happier to see us go. When we arrived home there were people in the yard, people in the house moving furniture. In the house, the potty-chair lay just as it did in my 'dream'. My dad's uncle was helping them move.

"Where's ma?" I asked, all that time had passed and I still wouldn't call her mama. "She's gone...", he answered, ".. and she ain't never coming back!"

My stepmother had left, good for her. My little brother and sister were also gone. The only family setting I had known. I was both happy and sad. Happy because she was gone and I had grown to dislike her. Sad because, now that she was gone who would my father beat?

ANOTHER NEW FAMILY

It didn't take him long. A few days passed before he moved another woman in. The same woman he had in the house when my 1st stepmother was in the hospital. He wasted no time; he married my 2nd stepmother. My sister and I liked her, she was wild. She reminded us of our mother. As much as we liked her, we still wouldn't call her mama. She wasn't our mother. Giving my father's track record she wasn't going to be there long anyway.

By now my life was so miserable. I really think my father hated me. He was so hateful and mean. I spent most of my time daydreaming. Daydreaming of a pretty yellow woman. Someone being kind and loving to me. My yellow friend had no name or face. I would seek comfort in the depths of my imagination. I longed for that soft comforting touch.

After my grandmother's verbal bashing of my mother began to get stale and old, she started coming up with more ludicrous, outlandish things to say. Her verbal abuse grew more hateful and mean. She accused me of being a whore. I was only ten or eleven.

"The spirit give it to me..", she'd say, "..you go die!...", she snarled, "They go find you on the beach dead!" "They go find you dead before you turn twelve, oh yeah, grandmamma know, you just watch what I tell you!" That terrified me, I wondered why would she say that? "The spirit give it to me, you go have four babies, before you turn sixteen year's old!" She would taunt.

How could you love a child and tell them things like that. This type of talk was normal and was talked about amongst other people in the small town. Even the other church mother's from other churches jumped on the 'bash Danielle' wagon. You mean to tell me, that those old ladies had nothing better to do than to badmouth an eleven year old child. I proved them wrong. I am alive and well, and I only have one child. Whom I had after I turned twenty-one.

They didn't care about the damage they were doing to me. They were making me have hate in my heart. Hate for them and more important hate for myself. I wonder do they realize what they have done to me. I have carried that hate around for myself all these years. If anything was lost or misplaced they said I had it. If it turned up they said I put it back. I was miserable. If anything could've been said about me, it was said. If anything could have been done to me, it was done. Accused of being a whore and everything. They had no idea, I didn't do sex, sex was done to me.

My father, my 2nd stepmother and my sister and I, moved from the house we had lived in with my other stepmother. We moved into another small two-bedroom house. At first we were okay, my father spent more time in the streets and less time beating his wife and kids. We didn't stay beating free for long.

I walked to Mr. Beards, a store about three blocks from our house. I went for my dad, to get some sugar. Having money was uncommon to me. We didn't get gifts, money, nothing! We very seldom got any clothes. My great-grandmother was no longer with us, so no more trips to the mailbox. Anyway, while picking up the sugar, I bought myself two banana laffy-taffy. Mr. Beard had just giving me permission to come back in the store. I had been barred because I used to steal his empty pop bottles and sell them back to him for a dime. I ate one of the taffy while in the store. I only had two blocks to walk; I hurried and ate the second taffy, so I wouldn't get in trouble. Now why on earth would I be scared to eat a laffy-taffy?

Because I got beat for everything! Even being too skinny. This is true. By the time I reached the house, I had eaten the taffy and thought I was in the clear.

"What's that in your mouth?" My father snarled. He was always roaring like a big gorilla. He grabbed me by my face, stuck his big, black, ugly nose in my mouth.

"Nothing." I said. I was terrified, not thinking he could smell the banana.

"You lying!" My father said. He grabbed me by my throat and threw me across the room. I thought my back was broken. I had landed on the hard wood coffee table.

"A piece of laffy-taffy!" I said.

"Why you lie?" My father asked me. I thought he was going to kill me. He grabbed me by my throat again. This time slapping me in my face.

"I don't know!" I said. I knew he was going to kill me.

THE ULTIMATE BETRAYAL

That wasn't the first time he had thrown me across the room. He had previously threw me and I landed on top of a telephone, in the small of my back. But he had never beat me like this. Before he used cable cords, extension cords and sticks(not switches either!). This time he used his hands. After being tossed and choked and slapped. He took me and threw me on my bed and began choking me again, like I had witnessed him do all three of his wives. He was still slapping me around, on both sides of my face. After I got older, I used to tease and say 'he beat me like I was one of his wives'.

'Why doesn't he just kill me, and get it over with?' I thought. But he didn't, he'd let me live this time. He ordered me to stay in my room. My room, that's where I spent most of my time. Only coming out to pee. He accused me of being a problem child. He made me stay in there in that dark room, alone. It was like I was being sent to the dungeon. I believe my grandmother made him think I was evil, a slut and cursed. I was his own flesh and blood. He was too dumb and too easily influenced, to see that I was not evil, my spirit had been battered and brutalized. All I needed was love.

The beatings got worse and came more often. I never got a chance to see my mother any more. I was all alone now. My father wouldn't even let me visit my Aunt Ida anymore. I can remember sitting quietly, while my father bad-mouthed my mother.

"Your mama's a drunk!" He taunted,
"she drink whiskey for breakfast and
she eat the bottles for lunch!" He
said laughing. "Say it!" He said
pointing at me. "Say your mama's
a drunk!" I wouldn't say it. "Say it!"
He yelled. He could have killed me
but I wasn't going to say it. "Come
here!" He beckoned for my full
sister.
"Huh?" My sister said, unaware of
what to expect.
"Say 'your mama's a drunk'!" He
said, encouraging my sister to
point at me.
"Your mama's a drunk!" My sister
said, looking at me. She looked

back at my father for further
instructions.

"She drink whiskey for breakfast!"
He told her. My sister looked at
my father, she didn't want to say
it.

"Say it!" He yelled, "say 'she drink
whiskey for breakfast'..."

"She drinks whiskey for breakfast.."
my sister said.

"And she eat the bottles for lunch!"
He was looking right at me, with
an ugly grin on his face. "Say it!"
He tells my sister. I was devastated,
how could she say that about her
own mother.

"...and she eat the bottles for
lunch!" My sister said.

It was at that point that I felt isolated from the rest
of the family. I realized I was alone. My daddy kissed
my sister, rewarding her for her disloyalty.

"Come here, Danielle!" My father
said. I thought he was really going
to kill me this time, for sure. I
stepped forward with my sad
eyes, ready to take my punishment.
I was going to take this one like a big
girl. I was not going to betray my

mother.

"Cuff my pants.." he said. What a relief, I thought my life was over. I cuffed his pants. Just as I finished, my father kicked me away, like an old scraggly mutt.

THE BEGINNING OF THE END

My father's behavior had become erratic. He begin beating his third wife. His hatred for me also grew stronger. He tore a hole in the wall so he could watch me. I overheard him telling his wife that something was wrong with me. He probably got that idea from his mother. I was only a child. An unloved, motherless child.

My father moved us into a place with no gas and no heat. To keep warm, me and my sister would sleep in the clothes that we were going to wear to school the next day. Which often times, smelled of urine. This caused problems for us at school with the other children. They teased and taunted us. My sister was a chronic bed wetter, until she turned thirteen years old.

My father still had that big ass Great Dane. That

dog was mean just like my daddy. Scooby wouldn't let my sister and I in the house when my father wasn't home. We stayed outside for hours. In the snow to our knees. My father would laugh when he finally got home. I didn't understand my father, what the hell was so funny about that? I thought he was crazy.

His rages were out of control. He moved us back to New Port from Barton. He begin beating my 2nd stepmother really bad. He threw her out of the front picture window. I bet she felt the same terror the two before her felt.

The teacher's began to suspect something was not right in the home. They asked questions bout the marks on my body. I was so scared, I denied everything. I wasn't going to tell them white people my daddy beat me. I would have gotten beat even worse. I remember when the child protective people came to the house.

"Who is it?" I asked, when she
knocked on the door.
"Melissa Brown.." she said, "..can
I talk to you?" She came to the
door with two white police
officers. I cracked the door about
three inches.
"Hi, I'm Melissa.." she said, "..I'm
from child protective....." I slammed
the door in her face.
"I can't talk to you!" I said, I knew

daddy was go get me!
"I just want to ask you a few
questions.." she was shouting
because I had closed the door in
her face.
"My daddy ain't here!" I said, I ran
in the back room. They left but I
knew they would be back. I was in
trouble.

I was so scared. I had the bubble guts. I almost
shit on myself. I didn't tell those teacher's anything.
But I knew he was going to beat me anyway. He
wouldn't believe me, I thought I was going to die. He
would be home soon and they were coming back. I
had to leave, I had to get away. So I ran away. I was
eleven years old and I thought I was running for my
life.

I found myself running along side streets. I
thought about going back, but, it was too late. If he
had gotten back, how would I explain where I was.
This was it, there was no turning back. If I could just
get to Aunt Ida's house, I would be safe. It took me
about an hour to walk about six blocks. I was ducking
behind bushes. I got to the high school baseball field
and hid in the equipment shed for about thirty
minutes. I was hungry, I was thirsty and I didn't have
any money. I thought every car that drove by was my
father. Aunt Ida lived a few miles from town. I didn't
think I was going to make it. I felt like she stayed

millions of miles away. I took a drink from the water fountain and started running again. They were playing softball and never noticed me. I traveled behind buildings and in ditches. Ducking and dodging every car I could. I kept going until I found a familiar backyard. Aunt Ida had this one friend that kept a lot of mentally retarded people in her home. She lived on the corner at the edge of town. Aunt Ida's house was just about a mile away. I found myself in familiar surroundings, I had been in that backyard before. Ms. Dorothy was her name. I think I startled her a little bit when I peeked from behind the house.

"Baby?.." Ms. Dorothy said, I don't
think she knew who I was. "Hey little
girl.." she got up from her chair. Ms
Dorothy was a big woman, maybe
close to 350lbs. I didn't know whether
to run or answer her.
"Ma'am?" I said, she could barely
hear me.
"Come here baby, what you doing
back there?" she moved closer.
"Danielle, is that you?"
"Yes, ma'am." I had been crying.
She didn't know what to do, she
called Aunt Ida.

Aunt Ida and Ms. Dorothy talked on the phone for a while. I think Aunt Idadidn't know what to do. She tells me she thought some one was playing games with her. Aunt Ida and my father didn't get along. She once pulled a rifle on my father and my mother pulled him off the porch. He had a way of treating women. He could never bully Ida though, she didn't let any men run over her. Ida Mae was her name, but the called her Ida Jean, she was a country girl with a city girl attitude. She wanted to speak to me.

"Hello..." I said.
"Danielle?" She said.
"Ma'am?" I began to relax and
almost felt safe when I heard
Aunt Ida's voice.
"Are you okay?" she asked.
"Yes, ma'am."

I could tell by the way she was hesitating she didn't quite know what to say. I know Aunt Ida, so I know she wanted to throw caution to the wind and come rescue me. That wouldn't have been wise and could have led to more problems.

"Ms. Dorothy is going to call the
police." She told me.
"You can't come and get me?" I
asked.
"We go call the police first", she
said, "and when he gets there,
we'll go from there okay?"

"Okay." I said, Aunt Ida knew best, and I trusted her.

Aunt Ida was so upset, she told me she wanted to run to my aid, but the way my father acted, it would have open up a can of unwanted worms. Ms. Dorothy called the police. The police came and picked me up. Ms. Dorothy gave the police officer money to take me to get something to eat. On the ride I sat in the back seat, I sat down really low so no one could look in the police car and see me. I spent several hours at the police station. I didn't care, at least I wasn't at home getting beat.

Aunt Ida was a foster mother, so they allowed me to stay in her home until it was time for court. When I arrived at Aunt Ida's house that night, she had some chicken noodle soup waiting on me. Chicken noodle was my favorite and Aunt Ida knew it. I took a warm bath. I laid down in the t.v. room. She had the hideaway bed ready for me. I didn't rest much that night. I had to face my father the next morning. I felt safe, if only for one night.

After all the brutality and all the beatings, the state turned me right back over to my father. My father despised me now, I had embarrassed him. It took me the longest time to get the courage to run. No one helped me, not even the police. I not only was a liar, a whore and a thief in my family's eyes; I was a black sheep and a traitor. Everyone blamed me.

What confidence and self-esteem I did have left,

was gone. My father beat me with an alarm clock cord, from Cable to Able Street. He told me to tell the police that.

My father was a vulture, he preyed on people's weakness, especially woman. Through other people's weakness, he found his strength. He didn't posses the financial stability or the emotional stability of the other family members, so he was considered a failure. He believed what they said about him and that made him weak. Someone should have told him that hate and brutality are improper ways to raise a family it takes love and understanding. Someone has since told me, my father was doing cocaine and taking Prozac. That may explain his violent rages, it could also be just a rumor. Who knows?

THE END

My father decided that he didn't want me anymore, so he sent me to live with my mother. My father put me on the bus. He didn't inform my mother of my arrival. I had to sit in that bus station for hours with no supervision. He sent me with no money. He sent me with no food. If you are familiar with the downtown bus station's in this country, during the early eighties, then you know that was no place for an eleven year old child. I knew I could call Aunt Ida.

"Hello?"
"Hello, this is the operator, I have a
collect call from Danielle, will you
accept the charges?
"Huh? " Aunt Ida said, she thought
someone was playing on the phone.

"Ma'am will you accept the charges?"
"Yes..." Aunt Ida said. "Danielle...
where you at?"
"Smithville.." I told her.
"Smithville?...what are you doing
there?" She asked, she sounded
confused.
"Daddy sent me." I told her.

The bus station was huge. My father should have
been ashamed of himself. That was no place for a
little girl. All this could have been avoided if he had
used his heart instead of his hands.

"Oh my God!" Aunt Ida said,
"where's Delores?"
"I called and she's not there." I
told her.
"Give me the phone number off
that phone and don't move.
"Yes ma'am." I said.

How could he do that to me? If he loved me or
had any feelings for me, he wouldn't have thrown me
away like that. I was convinced that he didn't care.
Aunt Ida taught me to always, no matter what
happened I should always love and respect my
father. I hated him from that point on. If he died that
day, I wouldn't have cared. He had thrown me away. I
was eleven years old and all alone in this big city.

After about twenty minutes the phone started ringing. It was my Aunt Ida.

"Hello?" I answered.
"Danielle...I talked to your mother." My mother was home when I called, she just didn't answer the phone.
"Is she go come and get me?"
"She's waiting on her ride."

It shouldn't have taken that long. I would have ran to my sons aid. Aunt Ida tried to console me and stop me from being scared. It didn't work, I was scared out of my mind. You should have seen all the freaks hanging out down there. All those strange looking people hanging around. Dope heads. Whores. Rapists. Killers. All this was running through my mind at the time. I was too young to deal with that. They have since cleaned up the down town bus station. It was a mess, when I was stranded there twenty-one year's ago. Aunt Ida instructed me to stay by the phone. I didn't move. For hours, I didn't move.

When my mother arrived that morning, she had been drinking. I had waited in that bus station for her for four and a half hours. I arrived at 8:30pm, she didn't pick me up until after 1:00am. Although she was already drunk, she told her old man she needed another drink.

"What you want Delores?" Fred

asked. Fred was my mother's
broke down sugar daddy. Even
though he was broke and had a
wife, he truly loved my mother.
"Gimmie the strongest drank they
got!" My mother told him.

Fred came out of the liquor store with a bottle of
'rock gut'. Three minutes after downing it, she was
throwing it back up. I witnessed her almost puke her
guts out, literally pissie drunk. I was embarrassed of
her and my embarrassment hurt my feelings. She was
my mother, I should've loved her unconditionally.

Although my mother loved me, she was no way
capable of raising me and taking care of me. She
didn't want me, we barely knew each other. I mean, I
knew of her, but that was it. My mother had five kids
and she ended up giving us all away. For years we
didn't acknowledge each other. Can you imagine
being in the same room with your siblings, knowing
there your siblings and not be able to speak on it?
Her drinking was terrible, way out of control. She
wasn't eating the bottles for lunch, but she was sure
drinking for breakfast, lunch and dinner. I couldn't
stay there. My father had shipped me to Smithesville
illegally. I wasn't supposed to leave the state, per
court order. I stayed a few days with my mother then I
returned to New Port. My father lost parental rights.
That suited me just fine. If I never seen him again, it
would be too soon.

I was now a ward of the state. I was placed in Aunt Ida's foster home. I felt safe. Although the beatings stopped and the majority of the molesting was behind me, the damage had been done. My family frowned down on me. Like I had did something wrong. My father denied that he ever mistreated us. He's a liar. I got beat almost every day of my life, between the ages of five and eleven. The only time I didn't get beatings was when, I was staying at Aunt Ida's house. I still have scars on my body from those beatings. Sometimes when I talk to my full sister, she helps me realize that I didn't imagine it. It really did happen. We kind of laugh about it now, but sometimes it makes us sad.

I had only been back from Smithesville about two weeks, when Aunt Ida's brother-in-law took advantage of me. He was maybe sixty year's older than me. That was the incident that stayed with me. I felt like it was my fault because it stimulated me. I can remember wanting to lie down. It felt good to me. I was only twelve year's old. He said we couldn't lie down because 'it might go in'. To this day it makes me sick to my stomach. I felt like a cheap whore.

After all the beatings, after all the molestations and after all the verbal abuse, my spirit and self worth had been stripped. My innocence lost. My family had cast me out, I never wanted that. I longed to be a part of my family. The fact that I ran away and embarrassed the family name stayed with me. The adults knew my family didn't want me. The children knew too. Not only was I not a recognized member of the family, I didn't have the protection that was given to every other Hamilton. I was frowned upon, talked about and ridiculed. Not only by strangers, but also by my own family. I am not exaggerating either. The very thing that they stood for, they neglected. Me, their family. My little sister trying to get on their good side, even lied to the teacher's and every body at our school, saying that I was pregnant. I hadn't even started my period yet. She was only doing to me, what they were doing to her. My full sister says they were trying to turn us against each other. We looked at each other with hate and disgust, instead of love.

Of all the people to accuse of fathering this baby, they chose Aunt Ida's husband. They said she had me at her house, so her husband could go with me. He tried to fondle my breast, once when I was fifteen. He was man enough to say he was wrong, and that he was sorry. I forgave him. Other men had done me worse then he and got away with it. He never tried to touch me again. He has been nothing but good to me. When my father decided to sit this one out, he stepped up to the plate and performed very well.

I was being talked about all the time. I had just turned twelve, and every week it was something. 'Danielle's pregnant' or 'Danielle's a lesbian'. I got so tired of hearing that. I knew nothing about being with another woman. I had fantasized about it, but never acted on it until I was twenty-two year's old. Isn't it amazing how people can be up lifted, by another person's downfall?

A NEW BEGINNING

I was an average teenager. I did things a teenager did. With the help of my Aunt Ida, I began my long uphill battle of recovery. It wasn't easy, I'm still recovering to this day. How do you repair years of physical and sexual abuse? Their is just too much damage to erase. My childhood had been destroyed. Neither Aunt Ida, nor myself could go back and fix it. My reality was so dark and filled with despair. I only found happiness in my daydreams. Day dreaming of a soft beautiful woman. I day dreamed so much, I was out of touch with reality.

Everybody knows that kids can be cruel. They teased me because of my Holland City mission clothes. I wore polyester two-pieces. Plaid pleated skirts and sweaters. Aunt Ida did what she could. She did what no one else wanted to do. I am thankful.

Most kids didn't accept me. I didn't quite fit in. I had friends, but I had no true friends. I don't talk to any of the people I went to school with. I felt so incomplete. I never had a boyfriend. Not because I wasn't good looking. I was afraid. I couldn't trust them. I was having intimate feelings, feelings I was taught were forbidden. Feelings that would send me to hell. That's what I believed. To this day I have a hang up with my sexuality. But I don't feel like I can ever be truly happy, with a man.

Aunt Ida loved me. She just ruled her home with a very strict, Christian backbone. I didn't mind that, at least I was safe from physical and sexual abuse. There was just no music, no videos, no phone calls and no boyfriends. I definitely didn't act on my attractions for girls.

I often watched video's when Aunt Ida went to church during the week. I also had a secret stash of my favorite music cassettes.

I had developed a complex. I didn't trust anybody. I felt like everybody was out to get me. I did trust Aunt Ida. Maybe I was a little paranoid. I was a lot like my father.

I didn't see much of my family for the next two years. That didn't stop them from talking about me though. I didn't see my mother for a while either. My grades where poor. It sucked to be me.

My full sister was now feeling the heat. They couldn't direct the verbal abuse towards me, I wasn't there anymore. My sister was now the target of the taunting and verbal abuse that I had once endured. She was a whore, she was pregnant. My grandmother was so negative. Why did she have to raise us. It wasn't her job. My sister tells me our grandmother was so twisted, she made my sister believe she was pregnant, before she had even started having sex. She tells me how she had to wear a t-shirt, sock or anything during her menstruation. Her entire menstruation. No pads, no tampons, no instructions. She was on her own.

I loved my sister, but I couldn't help feeling as I had gotten some form of revenge. After all the years of verbal and physical abuse my sister had helped put me through, I was glad that she was getting a taste of her own medicine. When I heard of my sister's mistreatment, finding out that I was, in fact, living a better life than she was, I felt better about my situation. I wanted my sister to hurt like I had hurt.

I had survived my grandmother's sick revelation. Not only had they not found me dead by the beach at twelve year's old. I was sixteen and had no children. I was beginning to feel like it was all bull. It wasn't meant for me. I just happened to get caught in the middle of another person's sickness.

"You can be anything you want
to be..." Aunt Ida would say,
"...anything!"

It didn't happen over night, but I was healing. I

had to talk to a counselor and a caseworker every week. I talked to my counselor about my hatred for my father. My inability to trust anyone. My counselor advised me to open up to Aunt Ida. I told her everything. She was appalled by what she heard. As hard as it was to believe, she believed me and felt my pain. Between the ages of five and fifteen, ten men and three women had molested me, over twenty-five times. That's not including what I can't remember.

I wasn't a perfect child. I had done things throughout my high school years. Petty theft, vandalism and I even had some destructive behavior. I pushed one of Aunt Ida's clients into a glass door. That retarded lady had to have about fifty stitches. I have asked the lord to forgive me for that every day. I also stole Aunt Ida's landlords' checkbook. Not only did I cash a check, I gave them to my so-called friends. I also set Aunt Ida's house on fire when I got kicked off the bus, after my cousin Cina had picked a fight with me. She beat me up really good. I got caught when I stole those checks. It broke Aunt Ida's heart to admit she knew I did that. She didn't whip me though. She probably should have. I straightened up after that. For a little while at least. They almost sent me to a detention center. Aunt Ida wasn't having it.

I didn't want my grandmother to be right about me. I wasn't a petty thief. I wasn't a whore. I wanted to be better than they thought I was. I wanted to prove them wrong. I learned my lesson fast. If I want something, I will work for it. No one's going to take care of me. I developed a need to be independent, I never wanted to have to ask anybody for anything. But stealing wasn't going to be my way of obtaining things.

My father must have misunderstood the bible quote, if your right eye offends thee, pluck it out. If your left hand offends thee, cut it off. He said that just before he sent my sister to live with Aunt Ida. Saying he would never fool with her again. I strongly feel that my grandmother urged this on.

Aunt Ida opened up her heart and her home. My sister and I, after years of separation, were together again. I began having adjustment problems. I started hanging with the wrong crowd. I begin to cut class. I would skip school and smoke weed. I got C's, D's and F's. I failed algebra two times. My home life wasn't going too well. I wasn't doing the right thing and Aunt Ida got kind of hard on me. The harder she chastised me the less I tried. Aunt Ida was particular to her son. I was eleven years older then he. She had gone all those years and treated me like her real daughter. Then it started to be all about him. I understood that. It's different when it's your real child. We couldn't eat his cereal. He was a spoiled little brat. I was a little jealous of him. I know Aunt Ida loved me. I just think she loved him more. Anyway, school wasn't going too well either. I couldn't apply myself. My high school class had approximately one hundred and eighty five students. My academic rank was one hundred and seventy eight, I believe. I had the potential to get all

A's. At the time, I had the ambition of a slug. That's how I went to school...sluggish. I did just enough to keep her off my back. I did it though. I got all the credits I needed and graduated. Barely. I was seventeen when I graduated.

It was a sunny Sunday. Weather in New Port is nice around that time of the year. I thought I was the bomb. Had my new outfit on. That was my day. My father didn't come. I guess I should have invited him. My mother had over indulged in a gallon of bumpy face and got lost. Although she had driven to New Port a hundred times, she got lost. That disappointed me. When I was getting ready, I thought it was one of the best days of my life. I had finally accomplished something. Even though I didn't invite my father, I wanted him to come anyway. I don't think he cared whether I graduated or not. He didn't believe in me.

Aunt Ida had went all out for my graduation. She fixed a feast. Dressing, ham, greens, macaroni and cheese. The works.

I have never been afraid of hard work. I always had a job. I worked real hard the summer before my senior year. So that I could purchase my senior pictures and class ring. Aunt Ida helped me with my senior package: cap, gown, invitations, etc.

My sister was helping me do my hair, when she let it 'slip' that my mother wasn't going to make it. First she was like 'she coming, she coming' then she had this devilish smirk 'she ain't coming, she ain't coming'.

My mother didn't even call. My sister has ways like my grandmother. Always had some shit going. My feelings being hurt entertained her. It was only an hour and a half drive from Smithville to New Port. She could have made it; she should have made it. My other family from Smithville made it. My aunt, my uncle's and my cousins. I thought I was so pretty. I felt special. My parents were no where around to share it with me.

I worked very hard my senior year, to make up for the first three years I slacked off. I went on to my graduation without my mother or my father. After the ceremonies we came home. There was a house full of people. Some where there for support, others were there taking up space. My 1st stepmother had the nerve to show up. My father's sister-in-law came with her. I overheard them in the kitchen talking about Aunt Ida's food. My stepmother said something like, 'the dressing needed some salt'. That pissed me off. I knew they weren't there for me. I wanted to tell them uppity hens not to eat it then! I wanted them to get the hell out! They didn't even bring me a gift. They meant me no good. They were also on the side of those who said I wasn't going to amount to anything. My stepmother wasn't even part of the family anymore. My aunt hadn't spoken to me in years. I was very angry. My anger didn't have much to do with them. It had a lot to do with the absence of my mother and father.

LOST

I was just as troubled, as a young lady, as I was as a child. I didn't have a clue, as to, what direction I was to go. I didn't know whether to go to school or get a job. With no support and no one to guide me, I was lost. I needed guidance and encouragement. I needed discipline too. So I signed up for the army. What a bad idea. I wasn't going to be all I could be. I was trying to get away from the town I hated so much. I had no roots there. I had a family, but I wasn't apart of it. There was nothing for me there. So I left. After I signed up for the army, Aunt Ida decided to move away too. She had suffered enough ridicule and humiliation behind taking care of me. No one wants to stay in a place where they're not wanted.

Signing up for the military was a big mistake. I

didn't want to be a soldier. I was running from something or to something. I have no idea. I wasn't at peace, my spirit was in turmoil. I needed fixing, but I didn't know how. I spent most of my free time in my room, in the dark, with the door locked. I was depressed all the time. I missed Aunt Ida. I wanted to go home. This white soldier told me I was too black and they put nazi signs on my door. I didn't have to leave home for that shit. I knew I couldn't hang. I stole one of the soldier's phone card and called home everyday. I ran his bill up to $200. I got wrote up for that. I was so embarrassed, I begged the first sergeant to let me go home. So 'for the good of the army', I received a 'general under honorable conditions' discharge. Once again I had no where to go. I called Aunt Ida, she had my back. Again.

Aunt Ida was now living in a small southern town. Aunt Ida's life was unhappy. She was married to a man who had a reputation of being fresh with the ladies. With the younger ladies. I don't know if Aunt Ida had ever gotten over him trying to fondle me. Chase was no better then New Port. No real jobs. No real opportunities. Aunt Ida's husband could be a mean and selfish man at times. If he felt like cutting off the air conditioner in 95-degree weather, he did. There was no communication between Aunt Ida and her husband. They didn't even sleep in the same bed. Aunt Ida had obvious reasons for that.

My sister had turned into a wild woman. She was always getting into fights. She had moved to Chase with Aunt Ida. She was acting just like a wild women. She had developed 'loose' behavior. She wanted to spend her time in the streets, drinking and partying. I love my sister, but she was awful in her younger days. My sister also had an uneasiness about her. I didn't understand till years later what she was going through. She ended up pregnant at the age of fifteen.

After I got home from the army, Aunt Ida moved us kids back up North with her. It was May or June when we moved back to New Port. When we got to New Port, my sister went crazy. She was maybe five or six months pregnant. She loved to party and go dancing. Things were still the same. People were closed minded. They still thrived on the negativity and downfalls of others. This was the worst year of my adult life. My family didn't welcome me back with open arms. In their eyes I was still nothing and a nobody. I stayed anywhere I could. Where ever I could lay my head. I really didn't have a place to stay for the first three months. The same two people that talked about me the most were in a boat worse than mine. They were full time crack addicts. That didn't matter, they still talked about me.

We hadn't had much contact with our mother. I hadn't seen her in about two years. The last time I had seen her, she was drinking and tried to fight my sister and I. I don't remember what exactly we fought over, we were dysfunctional teenagers with smart mouths and bad attitudes. But we didn't speak for two years. I can't believe I wasted all that time. I should have been there for her. She should have been there for me.

My sister begin having contact with her first. She went to stay with her for a week or two after we came back. My mother had gotten sick while she was with her. They had to call the ambulance. My sister says our mother's eyes were rolling back in her head. My mother had been drinking hard for a few year's then. I remember the day my cousin came and told us our mother was sick.

We were walking up the street to our father's sister's house. We stayed there a few nights. That was nice, she let up sleep on her floor sometimes. Anyway, my cousin had been looking for us. I knew something was wrong, she had a funny look on her face.

"Mama called..." she said.
"What's wrong?" I asked her, she
kind of hesitated.
"Aunt Delores's sick, mama said
if ya'll ever want to see your
mama alive again, you all need
to do it now!"
"What's wrong with her?" we asked.
"She's sick, ya'll need to go to
Smithville!" My cousin was acting
kind of strange.

We didn't know how bad my mother really was.

Our mother had a habit of not being 100% truthful all the time. She was known for storytelling. She had told my father a few years earlier, that I had gotten in a car crash and killed myself and my half-white sister. It didn't matter, we were going to see about our mother.

My father's nephew was on the corner playing craps with his crack dealing homies. I figured I would ask him to help me. We weren't close and barely talked. But I thought because we were cousins, the bullshit didn't matter. I needed his help, and I thought he would help me.

"Pooh-pooh.." I called his name.
"What?" He snarled.
"My mama's sick...can you take
me to my Aunt Ida's house?"
"Naw!" He said, he didn't even
look up at me.
"But my mama's sick, she finna
die!" I told him.
"Nope! trouble follows you." He told me.

Yellow motherfucker! I was crushed. They always pretended like blood was thicker than water, it wasn't. There was more trouble following him, then there was following me. And his trouble followed him all the way to the state penitentiary.

"Pooh-pooh, please!" I begged him.
"Nah, nope!" He continued to play craps.

I never forgave him for that. That really hurt me, it stuck with me for years. Some may say that was petty, but, that meant a lot to me. I was trying to see about my mother.

I walked the seven blocks to Aunt Ida's house. She didn't give it a second thought.

BAD NEWS

My sister, my two cousins and I, went to Smithville. My older cousin drove while we drank beer and smoked weed. By the time we got to the hospital, I was loaded. Higher than a kite! I was so nervous about seeing my mother. I didn't know what to expect. All the reefer in the world couldn't prepare me for what I was about to see. When I walked in the room, I almost fainted. I just fell back against the wall. My mother used to be the life of the party. Here she lay, hanging on to her life by a thread. Death was all in her face. She had developed disease of the liver, pancreas and spleen. Even as she lay there, barely alive, she begged for the very thing that had put her there in the first place.

I had to leave the room. I couldn't keep my composure. My high was completely gone. My mother was in agonizing pain. The doctors wouldn't give her any painkillers, her kidneys couldn't take it. They gave her a 30% chance of survival.

My mother couldn't get a liver transplant, because she was an alcoholic. She knew she was sick. The doctor said she had missed two years of appointments. She had also called us, almost two years to the day, saying she was going to die. She said the doctor had told her. We thought she was playing. She wasn't playing this time, she just told us she was. She recanted her story, I guess she didn't want us to worry.

After her chances dropped to 20%, her siblings decided not to make her suffer. Over a period of three days, we watched her die. I remember the last conversation I ever had with her.

"Help me, help me!" My mother was screaming, twisting and turning. I asked her what was wrong. She was pulling at the catheter. She looked bad, they had tubes all in her. She was in the intensive care unit. I told her she needed to leave the catheter in her, so she could get better. I was lying, I knew she wasn't going to make it through this.
"They said I was going to die!"

she said.

"Who?" I asked her, that broke
my heart to hear her say that.

"The nurse." She said, I was
angry, even though she was
dying, the nurse had no right!

"It's burning, it's burning!" She
was still tugging at the tubes.

"Oh mama..." I could hardly
speak.

"Go and get me some warm...
no, make it cool water, and
put it on my pussy!" She was
tossing and turning and tugging.

I wanted to help her, but what could I do? I had
never seen anything like that before. I had never
seen no body die. Those were the last words my
mother ever said to me. She passed away two days
later.

With my mother's death went many unanswered
questions. We would never know why she just gave
us away. My family was in an uproar. Things got ugly
between some cousins and myself. What the hell
were we fighting over? Who knows! What ever it was
I can bet it wasn't important.

I was affected by my mothers death more than I
let on. I was angry with her for giving her children
away. She should have kept us together. She had
taken away from us, the right to know each other. I

blamed my father for her death. At the time, I felt if he would have treated her better, maybe she wouldn't have drank herself to death. There was nothing any one could have said to make me feel different. If I was going to blame someone, it may as well have been him.

08/05/90

Dear mama,

How could you leave us? And the way you left everything. We needed you to take care of us, you didn't. I may never know my siblings on a personal level. You've made it difficult for me to walk in a room where they sit. The problem started way before your drinking. You can't help what happened to you as a child, but as you got older, you could have changed things and taken care of your responsibilities. Didn't you learn anything from your own experiences? Did you even care? Why didn't you stand up for us? Why weren't you there? I can't see what I could be, I only see what I am. Your unwanted child.

I missed your love when I was growing up. I cried for you at night. I longed for a hug and a kiss from you. I've never experienced a mother's love. You never took the time to tell me you loved me.

You knew you were gonna die, you told us. You should have taken those two years to fix things, get things right with your children. But instead, you choose to keep drinking. I don't want to stay here, I want to be with you.

09/05/90

Dear daddy,

I hate you! You killed my mother. You're the meanest, the blackest man I know. My mother lay dead, and you still breathe. I know you didn't make her drink, but you aided in making her hate herself. You are just as responsible for her death, had you shot her in the face. If you had loved your family, maybe things would have been different. Maybe she'd still be alive. Not only have you messed up your life, but you've messed up my life. You were mean and cruel. You were supposed to protect your family, instead you let them be slaughtered. Why didn't you protect me? How could you laugh and say it was my fault. How did you expect for me to love you and you didn't love me back? How could you call her a whore? You have more children then she does. It's your fault I have brothers and sisters I don't know. I could stand face to face and not recognize a part of me. My childhood has been a burden to me and it's all your fault. I will never forgive you.

My sister felt like I shouldn't have been hurt, because I didn't know her. I didn't have to know her, she was my mother. She gave birth to me. People tell me my mother didn't want me. I don't know if that's true or not. She probably didn't, she was still my mother.

Six months after she died, my mother's death was still fresh on my mind, and in my soul. My life was more confusing than ever. Me losing my mother did something to me. I think it had more to do with her giving me away. I was angry, angry with my father, angry with my mother, angry with myself.

BLESSING IN DISGUISE

Year's prior to my mother's death, I was just as promiscuous as my sister. Not to the extreme as her. But we were both having a lot of unprotected sex. I don't know about her, but I wasn't having sex for myself. I would cry and want them to hurry up and finish. They didn't care about me, I didn't care about me either. The majority of them I never communicated with again. I always felt like a slut afterwards, ashamed of what had taken place.

Most of my sexual experiences occurred between the age of fifteen and twenty. I never enjoyed sex with guys, until after I had been involved with a woman. Most times I had sex against my will. I didn't know how to stand up for myself or how to say 'no'. I didn't know all of the men I had sex with. I had sex with a couple men I had just met. Not even knowing their names. I didn't know I could say no. No one ever taught me. I grew up thinking that men could do what ever they wanted to me.

I met my 'baby daddy' two-year's before my mother died. He lived in the same town my Aunt Ida moved to when I went into the army. He was a country boy. Not drop dead gorgeous, but he was a sweet young man. I just didn't like him. Although I had sex with guys, I wasn't attracted to any of them. Because of my families' belief, I pretended to like guys. My child's father and I were never intimate until my mother passed. We hooked up when I drove to Smithville with a friend. The only reason I slept with him was so I wouldn't have to sleep in the cold truck again. It was an awful sexual experience. I cried and looked to the ceiling wondering how I let myself get in this situation again. I promised myself I would never do this unless I wanted to. My mother's favorite song began to play on the radio, 'Always and Forever'. My thoughts went to my mother's face and my yellow dress we buried her in. My mother's skin looked so dry. They buried her in her glasses and her false teeth. I never understood that, she never wore her teeth when she was alive, why would they make her wear them in death. She probably cursed us out for that. I began to cry, I missed my mother. I felt like I was doing the same thing that she did. Letting this man use me. I couldn't go through with it. I told him to stop. Without any hesitation, he got up. He didn't pressure me. I still hated him for not noticing how much I disliked it. Out of all the times I had unprotected sex, I never got pregnant. But this time, even after no climax was reached, I ended up pregnant. He denied being the father of this child. I understood that. He was ignorant to the fact that you don't have to have an orgasm to father a child. All it takes is a drop.

I wanted all my children to have the same father. If I couldn't have anymore children with him, I didn't want them with anybody.

The town jumped on my pregnancy, like flies to shit. Everyone had his or her idea about who my baby's father was. I knew who he was, to the contrary of what people believed. Here I was pregnant and alone. I had no job, no money and no place to live. I must have been crazy to let that happen, what was I thinking. I wasn't welcome in many households. I slept in cars. Aunt Ida didn't have a place of her own. Things were bad for the both of us. Aunt Ida was staying with her sister. Aunt Ida's crack addicted nephew didn't want me staying at his mother's house. So I slept in Aunt Ida's car. I was eight months pregnant and sleeping in a 1983 Chevy Chevette. No one had love for me but Aunt Ida. I knew I had to make a change or I would end up just like my mother. I had to leave that dreadful town and better myself. Soon I would have a child to look after. Aunt Ida and me loaded up that chevette and left New Port for good this time. Through the year's Aunt Ida would visit. I never wanted to go back.

I had a baby boy a month after we left town. I loved my son, but I just wasn't ready to be a mother.

Aunt Ida helped me with emotional support. When I decided to go to college she was right there and helped me with my son. I have never hired a real baby-sitter. Although she wasn't my biological mother, she treated my boy like her own flesh and blood.

COMING OUT THE CLOSET

College was a learning experience for me. Meeting new people, learning new things. I learned more non-educational then educational. My college years were full of good times. By now my attractions for woman were in full swing. If I didn't get a chance to act on them, I would explode. I had never acted on it, I just thought about it all the time. I had been fantasizing about woman since I was around seven. Out of fear of rejection, I suppressed those feelings. At first they were infatuation and small crushes. They soon turned into all out lust. My desire for women almost cost me my high school career. You can't spend your entire English and Algebra period fantasizing about women with hairy legs, in jet-black stockings. I didn't learn about weed in college that was something I had experienced at the age of twelve with my older first cousin. I mastered the art of smoking weed, in college. One would think I was going for a Ph d in cannabis.

I met and became friends with people that I was comfortable and could be myself around. I hadn't told anyone of my true feelings, I never even admitted it to myself. For some reason I felt free, maybe because I was in a new city, with new people. No one knew my past or me. That meant no one could hold my past or my mother's sins against me.

I had developed a crush on a nursing student. She was a nice lady. Almost ten-years my senior. We became good friends. I had never had anyone besides Aunt Ida to go out of his or her way to be nice to me. Aunt Ida was not an affectionate woman, this nursing student was the first woman to show me affection. Prior to this experience, anybody that showed me affection, was probably a pedophile. Their affections were coupled with molestations/perversions. After a few months of going to class and just hanging out, I began becoming aroused by her mere presence. I had also become friends with a young man who was on his way out of the closet. I confided in him of my feelings. He encouraged me to first make a play or flirt with her. It was such a relief for me to talk to him, and get those feelings off my chest. It didn't change how he felt about me. We became even closer.

My friend, the nursing student and myself, used to hang out between classes. Why we were smoking weed and drinking on the college campus is beyond me. I was really nervous, my friend tried to get me to tell the girl that I liked her.

"What ya'll doing this weekend?" He asked.
"Nothing.." I replied
"Ya'll want to kick it with me?" He asked.

He was eyeing me to say something. I was too scared to say anything. I had never acted on my attractions before. Every time I touched this girl's hand, a tingle would go up my back. Every time she gave me the blunt, I did everything I could to just brush up against her.

"I got to work this weekend." She said.
'Damn!' I thought. Maybe next time.

If this broad wasn't down, she sure didn't act like it. A female who's 'strictly dick-ly' would have warned me of her personal space. I felt as if I was on third base. I hadn't even started playing the game.

"She likes you!" He told me.
"No she doesn't!" I told him.
"Yes she does!" He told me.
"How you know?" I asked him.
"I can tell!" He answered.

You would think I had won the lottery. My friend and I, fully loaded, staggered in the building. I was so excited. I couldn't wait to see her again. This was my first lesbian experience. The beginning of my 'coming out'. I felt so free, and I thought I was happy.

I suppressed my pain and anger about my past, but there was never a day that I didn't think of my mother. I had no contact with my family, except my full sister. My sister was growing up too fast. I cut all ties to my family, I didn't write, I didn't call. I don't think they even missed me. I Probably never crossed their minds. I was starting over. New life, new beginning.

The nursing student was my first love, or my then interpretation of love. I had never really experienced love, I really had no idea what love was. She was somewhat homophobic, she lived in a really small town. She wanted to keep us a secret. I didn't care if she wanted it that way, I didn't want anybody to know I was like that either. I had just come out the closet. When rumors began circulating about the nature of our relationship, she couldn't take it and dumped me. My heart was broken, I thought I was in love. We really didn't have a real relationship anyway. She had another life that I couldn't be apart of. At the time, I was devastated. I later realized, I was more in love with her money. She had a nice job and she didn't mind sharing the wealth. She later came back to me. But when she first dumped me, I was crushed. I had met some friends who were all gay. This one girl, we called her Phat, was a ball player. She looked just like a lesbian. She was cool, but you could tell she was gay. I was afraid to go out in public with her because people would know I got down like that.

"Dawg, what's wrong?" Phat asked me.
"Nothing!" I screamed. I was drunk and
had just thrown a brick in my own car!
"Calm down!" Phat told me. I was gathering
some rope, a butcher knife and some
other stuff.
"That bitch ain't fucking with me any more!"
"Did you talk to her?" Phat asked. I had tried
to talk to her, she wouldn't talk to me. She
told me not to come around and just
slammed the door in my face.
"We go need to stop at the store and get
some duck tape." I said
"What the hell?..." she asked "...for what?"
"I'm going to kidnap her!" I told her.
"Oh my God!" Phat snickered, I had
really flipped. I was drunk.
"What? you ain't got my back?" I asked
"Yeah dawg, I got your..."

I didn't let her finish, I snatched Phat's keys and locked her and her girlfriend in the trailer. I had gathered some linen that I shared with this girl. Some clothes and things she had bought, piled it on the concrete in front of the trailer, soaked it in lighter fluid and set everything on fire. What a drunken fool! I then unlocked the door and passed out on the couch. That was my first heartbreak. I was young, thought I knew everything and I didn't have a clue.

I can't explain my lesbian lifestyle, not even to myself. Some days I don't have a problem with it. Sometimes I don't understand it. I feel like I've been looking for something. I thought the feelings I getting from the women was what I was looking for. I do know that I could never be completely happy with a man. My father was a very abusive man. His behavior left a permanent impression on me. I won't say all men are no good. The ones I've been around aren't. Although, I've never been involved 'intimately' with a man long enough to deal with his issues.

I feel like I can control my relationships with women. To me, all a man wants from me is sex. I see them as walking hormones. I'm not completely happy with women, but I'm comfortable. I think me not being completely happy with the way my life has turned out, plays a big part in the unsuccessfulness of all my relationships. I'll never forget the look on my friends' face, when I was asked if I was in love. My reply was a very cold 'I don't think so.' You should know when you're in love. I don't know exactly what love is. Being in love should touch my soul. I've never been emotionally touched, ever. I care deeply, just not as deep as needed. I have too many issues I need to deal with before I can make anybody happy.

Do I feel homosexuality is wrong? I don't know. I was taught that it was. I've prayed and asked God, if this is wrong, than take the desire away. The more I asked for the desire to be taken away, the more women come on to me. I have stopped myself from wishing for a 'normal' life. I must deal with what I have in front of me. I have to except my life and all that it entails.

My Aunt Ida doesn't exactly accept my lifestyle, she just deals with it. I wouldn't dare discuss it with her. I have too much respect for her.

It bothers me to deal with my paternal families' disapproval of my sexuality. Sometimes I'm even embarrassed by my lifestyle, especially when my father warns my sister to keep my niece away from me. He's afraid I'll molest her. He doesn't know me at all, that's disgusting! There's a difference between sexual preference and perversion. That's when I feel like I should follow the 'rules'. But I do understand that I must live my life for my son and myself, so I'll do what ever makes me happy. I'm uncomfortable when people stare and wonder 'do I get down?'. People accuse me of being confused. I'm not confused, I don't want to be a man. I wear Hanes <u>her</u> way, Victoria secrets, not BVD! I'm very much in touch with my feminine side. Sometimes my 'dyke' friends ride me for that. Calling me a 'fag' or 'fruit'. I'm satisfied with being a woman. I have a soft side, I love my toenails polished. I am woman hear me roar.

I spent the next couple of year's with a lot of different women. I thought I was a pimpstress, a female mack, Donna Juan. I thought I was happy, my life was coming together. I was getting an education and trying to find myself. Everything seemed okay on the outside, but I was dark underneath.

A BAD MOTHER

I loved my son, but at first I was a really bad mother. Crossing the line between discipline and child abuse often. He was only a child, I didn't understand what he needed. I was not ready. I found myself doing the same antagonizing and hurtful things to my son, that my father had done to me. Aunt Ida warned me to deal with my anger and hateful ways towards my son, before he would remember my mistreatment of him. I was angry with my child, angry about the love he had for my Aunt Ida. I was jealous. I didn't think he loved me. He never wanted to leave his grandmother's side. He didn't want to live with me, that hurt my feelings. So, I reacted to hurt with anger. I was actually too wrapped up in my new world to give him the proper care. I couldn't comprehend that Aunt

Ida was all he knew. When I realized that I was making my child hate me, just as I did my father. I changed my behavior. A child shouldn't be afraid of its parents. I was scared of my father. I don't remember ever running and jumping in his arms. I don't remember him ever putting his arms around me and telling me he loves me. I only have one fond memory of my father. I remember him playing with me at the beach. He pretended he was falling and I was in his arms. I was terrified. I thought I was going to drown. I was scared to swim for twenty-five years.

I was not going to let my child turn out like me, unloved and neglected. He didn't ask to be born, I was responsible for becoming pregnant. I wanted my child to love me, so I began to love my child. I learned to receive love, you must first give love. That's all everybody needs anyway. Love.

Problems don't go away. I suppressed the pain and anger. I never dealt with my issues, just bottled them up. I often wondered about my brother's and sister's. What was their upbringing like? How did it affect them? I never talked to any of my other siblings besides my full sister. I always felt like something was missing from my life. Like I wasn't quite complete. My family and emotional life was strained, but my social life was on the rise.

I found temporary fixes, which I thought filled the void in my life. I had unsuccessful relationship after unsuccessful relationship. My relationships were empty and meaningless. Some lasted a little more than three months, most lasted less. I had forgot what I was looking for in life. I got all wrapped up in the 'life'. My marijuana habit went from acute to chronic. Phat and I were smoking between one half an ounce and an ounce a day. I had stopped going to class and began getting lost in my daily routine. I was a pothead, a slacker. I smoked first thing in the morning and the last thing at night, and every time in between. All that mattered were women and weed. I wasn't just smoking to sooth my mind, I was overindulging. I needed it. I needed the women too. I thought I had found what my mother took with her when she left me. It made me feel good for the women to like me. But after the infatuation and the thrill was gone, the relationship could no longer camouflage the mess my life was in.

I think I have had more women then men. I've had women want to leave their husband to be with me. I've had my share, old ones, young ones, good ones and bad ones. I played the good ones and the bad ones...I was too paranoid to be played. You can believe the bad ones gave me a run for my money and my life.

There were only two bad ones. Nia and Leslie. Leslie was a real whore, when I met her she had a woman. I didn't care, I thought it was cool to be able to catch somebody slipping. I never intended on being with her, I just got caught up in the game. She taught me how a woman shouldn't behave. She wanted a Capt. sav-a-ho. All wrapped up into getting her hair and nails done. Sitting around waiting on her welfare check. I'm a strong believer in helping those that help themselves. She was looking for a free ride, I wasn't giving one, so she kept looking. It didn't hurt me when we broke up, I expected it. The way you get them is the same way you lose them.

Nia was a real lunatic. Let's just say after the one...no, two...no...three near death experiences, I was ready to give up my lesbian ways.

I decided to take a break, step back and take a good long look at my life. Decide how I wanted to spend the rest of it. I had gone trough a four-year shame spiral about my sexuality. I knew I was taught differently. I was taught homosexuality was an abomination to God. I hadn't given myself an opportunity to be in a heterosexual relationship, so I tried to relate to men differently. Although I found men attractive, I couldn't relate to them on a mental and emotional level. I soon learned that I could have sex with a man but not an emotional commitment. I knew it wouldn't be fair to be in a relationship with a man, I couldn't give them 100%.

MORE BAD NEWS

My faith in God was shaken. I didn't understand why he would let me be born in to this world destined to fail. I felt like I was in a no win situation. My belief was weak. I felt like God was giving me a life of unhappiness. I couldn't believe I was put on this earth to be molested and beat. I blamed God for my sorry, pitiful life. I was wrong.

I let the pain from my past rule my world. I gave it more power, than I gave myself. I held on to my past so tight, that it had begun to weigh me down.

One day I stood in the mirror looking myself over. I stood there a long time. I hated what I saw. I was disgusted with myself. My life was a waste. Twelve years had passed, and I was no closer to resolving the problems that I had ran away from. My living was in vain. If it weren't for my son, I would've given up. I had no other reason to live. All the anger and pain from my youth was suppressed. And allowed to fester. My pain had turned into hate. I hated my life, I hated my past, and I hated myself. I have been to the point where, I have slapped myself, punched myself. I have cursed myself. I could curse myself, better than my enemy ever could. I have called myself every name in the book, black bitch, fat bitch, dyke bitch, everything! I hated what I had become...nothing! All the college was a waste. All I'd accomplish meant nothing. All the jewelry, all the clothes, my good cars and the piece of crap I drive now, nothing! I don't lie about the things I have done. I've done some bad, mean, cruel things. But I am a good person. I am tired of being unhappy.

People are always telling me 'that's the past, let it go!' How can I let it go and I haven't even dealt with it. I've been so weighed down all these years. I've become comfortable with being unhappy. Then something happen to me, I developed fibroid tumors and cancer in my ovaries.

The night before my surgery, I sat and cried like a baby. I thought of my son, my Aunt Ida and all the unhappiness in my life. I was scared. I had 15 fibroid tumors. One the size of a football. I looked like I was eight months pregnant. All those years of not wanting another child, now I could no longer have another child. That saddened me. I still feel like God was punishing me for my lesbian ways. He blessed me with the ability to bring life, I didn't use it, and he took it away. I was afraid I might die. I prayed to God. I thanked him for my being. I thanked him for my family. I wanted God to forgive me for the hate I had in my heart towards my mother and my father. I promised never to call her a whore and a drunk again, I promised never to call him a black, ugly gorilla. I have did that over and over again. I am so ashamed. But I was angry with my parents. I still had no right. I believe my mother's spirit felt my hate. I also asked my mother for forgiveness.

I was willing to forgive my father too. I said when they cut out the sickness in my body, they where cutting out all the sadness and unhappiness. I was tired of carrying all that heaviness around. The surgery was successful, of course I survived. I was only to have a partial hysterectomy. My ovaries had swollen to the size of oranges and lemons, and filled with a chocolate-like fluid, so they had to take everything.

The next few months were hard, but I was happy to be alive. I couldn't work, I had no money saved. My financial failure caused me to lose my house. The surgery made me go into menopause. I dealt with a difficult bout with depression. I even contemplated suicide. Throughout my sickness I still smoked weed on a daily basis. Just as my past was weighing down on me, so was my weed habit. Weed may not be as bad as crack, it's still a drug and I was addicted. I didn't act like a junkie, but I still allowed it to smother my life.

MORE BAD NEWS

Ring, Ring....
"Hello?" I had picked up the phone
before I was completely woke.
"Danielle?" It was my full sister. It was
about 2:15am. That was not
uncommon. My sister called me in
the middle of the night, all the time.
"What?" I said
"Grandma is dead." She said
"Oh yeah?" I was woke now. And
thoughts were flooding my head. I
wanted to say 'so'. But it wasn't the
time.
"I'm go call you later." She said. My
sister must have sensed how I was
feeling.
"Okay, bye." I told her.

"My grandmother's dead...good!"
and went back to sleep.

The next morning it had almost slipped my mind, until my friend mentioned it. I debated if I should attend. My father told me I needed to be there at her funeral. I felt like she needed to be a better grandmother. My grandmother's death opened old wounds. I talked to my mother's sister about attending. She had harsh feelings about my grandmother. When I told her I was probably going to attend. She offered me $50 towards my trip.

"Fuck her!" She said, she meant that
too. She was upset about what they
had put her sister through.
"Don't be so mean!" My uncle told
her. My Aunt tactics amused me.
"Well.." My uncle said, "..tell the family
I send my regards."
"Okay." I said
"Well...you can tell them all I said 'to
kiss my ass!'" We laughed.
"Awwh Ippie, you a mess!" My uncle said.

I decided to go, because if I didn't go, my paternal family wouldn't let me live it down. I wasn't too upset about my grandmother's death, I could really have cared less. After all she had put me through, I felt nothing.

Things hadn't changed, they were still stuck up. They still acted like they were better than everybody. They weren't any better than anybody. They sin and have downfalls like everybody. They just know how to sweep it under the rug a little faster and better than some of us.

So much time had passed, years. I had changed, I was a grown women. I had no idea how much I had missed not being apart of my family. I needed that sense of belonging.

When I arrived at my grandmother's house, I was nervous. You could tell the house was full from all the cars out front. As I stood on the front porch, I grabbed the doorknob. I could remember as a child how my grandmother's door was never locked. I proceeded to enter without knocking, just as I had did a hundred times as a child. The house felt spooky, I hadn't been there in a long time. There were no pictures of my son or myself, on the mantle piece of the fireplace. I don't think they ever burned a fire in that fireplace. My younger brother was the first to embrace me. I hadn't seen him since he was a baby. He was a grown man. I wanted to cry, all those year's, all that space between us. One by one, my cousins begin to emerge from the back room. All those boys had turned to men. They gave me love. I hadn't seen most of them in fourteen years. And there sit my father, with his bad haircut and his cheap shoes. He never got up from his seat to embrace me, he just sit there plucking that cat-pickin' guitar. After standing there waiting for some love from him, I decided to go somewhere I felt comfortable. I wanted to find my younger brother, for him to make his way around everybody, and extend his arms like there wasn't an 18 year gap between us, brought tears to my eyes. I felt welcomed and loved with him.

Everyone except my father seemed pleased to see me again. They went on about how good I looked. How good I had turned out. Surprised to see me doing so well. What did they expect? For me to be a junkie or a whore?

The day of the funeral was a dark rainy day, kind of scary. All the family met at my grandmother's house. The house was full and quiet, no one said a word. My great uncle pulled me to the side, he wanted to have a word with me.

"Danielle?" He said
"Yes?" I said
"I just wanted you to know that not
everybody, threw you all away."
At first I thought 'God why is he
talking so loud'. He wasn't really
talking loud. I just felt uncomfortable
talking about my past.
"I tried to have you all live with
me, they wouldn't let you." He said
"I'm okay, it's cool, it doesn't
matter." I said.
"Well, I just wanted you to know

that not every body threw you
away!" He said
"It doesn't bother me." I told him.

I lied. It bothered me, it bothered me almost everyday. I wanted to break down and cry, right there in his arms. For him to acknowledge that I was thrown away, hurt my feelings. Surely, if he knew I was thrown away, others also knew. To me, it meant every one knew, but nothing was done. That was like pulling a scab off of a freshly healed wound. He felt bad? He felt bad, for what he seen. What about all the unseen? He had no idea, what I'd been through. I wanted to curse him. I wanted to tell him 'how dare you?' I wanted to tell him I didn't need him to apologize. I didn't need his pity, I didn't want it. I was a survivor and had survived. I was never going to be anybodies victim ever again. It was too late for 'I'm sorry'.

CLOSURE

My grandmother was put away nicely. She had on a white suit like she was pure. They painted a different picture of her. How spiritual she was, how loving she was, how much of a praying soul she was. No mention of all the gossip she started, or how many people she had talked about. They never said anything about her being two-faced either. I don't know what change occurred while I was away, but that wasn't the Grandma I knew. I wanted to jump up and scream 'I'm at the wrong damn funeral!' They said she was a saint, but I don't know. There was a thunder and lightning storm. The light's even went out in the church. At the burial site, the wind rose so high, it almost blew the canopy over. The grandmother I knew wasn't a sweet, cookie-baking grandmother.

She was a mean and evil old lady that talked about every body, I didn't know who the hell they were talking about.

The sound of my cousins playing the organ and strong, deep voice, reminded me of the days of my youth. The sunshine band and choir practice. It almost made me miss home. But there was too much bad blood. That wasn't my home. I didn't belong there. I didn't fit in, I was the prodigal child. After the service, which lasted for hours, my grandmother's children said their final good-byes. I was overcome with sadness to see the uncle that instigated many of my beatings, cry like a baby for the loss of his mother.

Most of my grandmother's children had done well for themselves. Strong black proud men in designer suits and driving Cadillac's, and their wives draped in expensive minks...and there stood my father in his cheap suit, looking sad and alone. It was that moment that I was willing to let go of the past and start over. I felt sorry for him. I too had lost my mother and felt his pain. I threw my arms around my father, tears running from my face.

"I'm sorry for your loss." I whispered.
He said nothing.
"I'm your daughter and I love you."
"I know." He said, cold and dry. His arms to his side.

He never put his arms around me. That's all I

wanted, it was all I needed. I probably could have walked away at that point and never thought of my past again. He never showed any emotion. I could have fell to the floor, my feelings were so hurt. I had put the hurt and anger aside, to console my father and he rejected me...again.

Although I hadn't completely let go of the hatred for my father, it had taken me twenty years to muster up enough love to hug my father's neck. It took him thirty seconds the tear it down again. I left New Port, and I swore never to go back. There is nothing for me to go back to. I am an adult now and I refuse to allow anybody to mistreat me. They don't know me, they have no idea how or why I live my life my way. I'm not the same troubled child my family shunned twenty years ago. I am a grown woman who should be commended on my survival. Not only had I survived my harsh upbringing, I was making it through life, which ain't easy. If my father doesn't want to embrace me fine. If my family doesn't want to embrace me fine. That will be their loss. I'm a caring, loving person, with a good heart. Being that I'm thirty-one year's old, I don't have time to spend another twenty year's weighed down with hate, sadness and despair. I have fifteen brothers and sisters. Probably over twenty nieces and nephews. Of whom all I need. Hopefully, they will need me too.

I have decided to change my life. From now on, I will never overindulge in anything other than my family. I will love my family, I will love myself. I will no longer feel sorry for myself. If I get all my brother's, sister's, nieces and nephews together, I will find the love I've been always searching for. All those year's I had felt alone. I wasn't. I pointed the finger, who did this and who did that to me. What is important is, what I do for myself. I must stop placing the blame and get on with my life. I wasn't the only child to be mistreated. If we don't do something soon, I most definitely won't be the last. Because...I'm just <u>one</u> of the lost souls.

MORE CLOSURE

Dear Grandmother,

Please forgive me for all the hate I have carried in my heart towards you. I don't quite understand your reasoning, but I forgive you. Thank you for the things you did do for me. You did take me in when my mother wasn't around. I do thank you, because you didn't have to extend yourself. I understand things weren't easy for you. I no longer hold you responsible. REST IN PEACE.

Your granddaughter,
Danielle

Dear Aunt Ida,

You're the only one that truly loved me. Thank you. Thank you for treating and loving my son, as if he were your own flesh and blood. Thank you for showing me, despite what people said, that I could do anything I set my heart to do. When I was hungry, you fed me. When I needed clothes, you bought them. When I needed refuge from the storms of life, you gave me shelter. You tried to make my life better, the best you knew how, and I thank you. You are one of the strongest women I know. When they talked about you and ridiculed you for helping me, you stood fast. Like a rock, unmovable. I thank you. To see you suffer, breaks my heart. To see you unhappy, breaks my spirit. How can someone who has helped so many, have it so hard. But you always keep going, never giving up. You may not have a lot of money, but you are rich in spirit.

You have showed me that family doesn't necessarily have to be blood related.

Forgive me for any and everything I have said or done to wrong you, in all of my lifetime. I'm sorry if I have disappointed you by not being successful. I hate to see you want for anything, I wish I could give you the world.

I love you, I love you, I love you more.

Your daughter,
Danielle

To my siblings,

Let's utilize the most important thing our biological parents gave us....EACH OTHER.

Love your sister,
Danielle

To my mother,

Please forgive me, for I know not your reasons. I forgive you too. I love you...REST IN PEACE.

Your daughter,
Danielle

To my father,

I forgive you. Even if you haven't asked for it. I love you, even if you don't love me back. I've learned a lot from you, like how not to treat my children. It's not to late for you, you can let go and embrace us. That doesn't make you less of a man. You'd be surprised how much better you would feel. I also ask for you to forgive me. Forgive me for the hatred that I have had in my heart towards you. Forgive me for the things that I have said or done to embarrass you, or disrespect you. That day that you couldn't find it in your heart to embrace me, will stay with me forever.

I no longer blame you for my mother's death. I apologize for that misplaced blame. All I ever wanted was for you to love me. But don't worry, I'll never ask again. It's a shame that I even have to ask. When I look at my son, and I feel that warmth in my heart, when he's at school and I wonder if he's okay, or when I worry about him, when he's playing with friends, I get a little jealous. He has something I have never experienced....a parents love.

Your daughter,
Danielle

EVEN MORE CLOSURE

I'm finished, I feel like someone has lifted a 10-ton truck off of my back. I can breath again.

Some people may not believe me and call me a liar. Some people may feel sorry for me. I'm not trying to convince anyone and I don't want pity. Everything I have put in this book, is the unadulterated truth. My reasoning for writing this book is not to throw stones. Those who played their part, know who they are. I don't have to prove anything, it's already been done. I wrote this book to somehow free myself.

My past has been like iron shackles. I have broken my chains. I hope my book helps someone else break theirs. Better yet, <u>prevent</u> them from even being put on.

I don't hate anyone. I no longer hold anybody accountable. I will not allow hate to hold me back anymore.

I have been afraid all of my life. Afraid to try, afraid to fail. I have isolated myself from others and the world. Fear will not ruin my life. My past is just that...my past. I will live my life here & now.

Forgiveness is a big part of healing. I have forgiven and in turn I will heal. I will learn to love, <u>unconditionally</u>. More important, I will learn to love <u>myself</u> unconditionally. I will, from this point on, live a happier, healthier life.

I don't know exactly where I go from here, probably no where. But in the words of ole' Ms. Celie, I may be poor, I may be black, I may even be ugly, but thank God, I'm free. I'M FREE.

ACKNOWLEDGEMENTS:

TIFFANY BOLDEN
LICRISSA MIMS
ANGELA STRONG
JACQUIE COUSIN

THANK YOU FOR YOUR SUPPORT & INPUT.